THE CURSE OF ILL TEMPER

THE CURSE OF ILL TEMPER

LESSONS FROM SCRIPTURE AND LIFE

T.M. FAUNCE

PRIMIX PUBLISHING

THE WRITE CHOICE

Primix Publishing
East Brunswick Office Evolution
1 Tower Center Boulevard, Ste 1510
East Brunswick, NJ 08816
www.primixpublishing.com
Phone: 1-800-538-5788

© 2026 T.M. Faunce. All rights reserved.

No part of this book may be reproduced, stored in a retrieval system, or transmitted by any means without the written permission of the author.

Published by Primix Publishing: 05/07/2026

ISBN: 979-8-89194-646-0(sc)
ISBN: 979-8-89194-647-7(e)

Library of Congress Control Number: 2026912739

Any people depicted in stock imagery provided by iStock are models, and such images are being used for illustrative purposes only.

Certain stock imagery © iStock.

Because of the dynamic nature of the Internet, any web addresses or links contained in this book may have changed since publication and may no longer be valid. The views expressed in this work are solely those of the author and do not necessarily reflect the views of the publisher, and the publisher hereby disclaims any responsibility for them.

The Destructive Power of Ill Temper

And he was angry, and would not go in: therefore, came his father out, and intreated him.
(Luke 15:28)

This passage highlights the curse of an ill temper, the folly of man. Since the time Cain killed Abel, this sin has remained one of the vilest forms of darkness, claiming untold numbers through its virus of hatred. In Luke chapter 15, the story of the prodigal son unfolds—a young man who gave himself to the lust of the eyes, the lust of the flesh, and the boastful pride of life. The father, more than willing to forgive, welcomes him back, but the older son becomes angry at his brother's restoration. Though commendable for his faithfulness and hard work, the elder son harbored anger and jealousy, refusing to join the celebration. The older sons, reaction likened to a spoiled child slamming doors when he does not get his way.

What causes quarrels and what causes fights among you? Is it not this, that your passions are at war within you? You desire and do not have, so you murder. You covet and cannot obtain, so you fight and quarrel. You do not have, because you do not ask. You ask and do not receive, because you ask wrongly, to spend it on your passions. (James 4:1-3)

I think we can all understand the sin of the elder brother, having themselves fallen prey to ill temper. This destructive force divides nations, fuels wars, and results in loss of life. Like a vile dragon, ill temper breathes flames of destruction, with rage as its only outcome. Anger brings forth ruin, just as a weed in a fruitful garden chokes out life, if not plucked out immediately. At its root, bitterness is pride—man's arrogance demanding his own way. The process of reflecting on this sin is painful, bringing conviction for past failures. Its effects are swift and merciless, like an out-of-control hurricane. Even those who weep sincerely in prayer can lash out in uncontrolled anger, undermining their own testimony. To truly honor God's calling, one must address and overcome this sin. Satan continually sets traps for the ill-tempered. ILL TEMPER CAN DESTROY A TESTIMONY IN SECONDS.

Be angry, yet do not sin." Do not let the sun set upon your anger, (Ephesians 4:26)

Pride and Spiritual Blindness

As she stood behind him at his feet, she began to wet his feet with her tears. Then she wiped them with her hair, kissed them, and poured perfume on them. When the Pharisee who had invited him to diner, saw this, he said to himself,

"If this man were a prophet, he would know who is touching him and what kind of woman she is—that she is a sinner."
(Luke 7:38-39)

The Example of the Weeping Woman

Here presents another contrast. A woman, weeping at Jesus's feet, washes them with her tears and anoints them with perfume. This scene is a powerful display of humility and repentance. In stark opposition stands the Pharisee, whose heart hardened by pride and judgment. While the woman openly acknowledges her brokenness and need for forgiveness, the Pharisee silently criticizes both her and Jesus, questioning His prophetic ability and the woman's worthiness. This moment illustrates how spiritual blindness, fueled by pride, prevents one from recognizing true grace and transformation. The humble posture of the woman is honored, while the self-righteous attitude of the Pharisee exposes his inability to receive or extend mercy. Such spiritual pride not only blinds individuals to their own need for grace but also causes them to judge and exclude others who seek restoration and healing.

Pharisee's Offense and Spiritual Blindness

The Pharisee who had invited Jesus to his home became offended as he observed the scene unfolding before him. Seeing the woman, known to be a sinner, weeping at Jesus's feet and washing them with her tears, he thought to himself that if Jesus were truly a prophet, he would recognize her sinful reputation. In his heart, the Pharisee questioned both the legitimacy of Jesus's prophetic status and the worthiness of the woman, allowing his pride and judgment to cloud his perception. This response reveals the Pharisee's spiritual blindness, as his self-righteous attitude prevented him from recognizing the genuine humility and repentance displayed by the woman, as well as the grace and authority embodied in Jesus. Instead of responding with compassion or understanding, the Pharisee's pride led him to silently criticize and exclude, demonstrating how spiritual arrogance can hinder one's ability to perceive and participate in the transformative work of God.

Two Responses: Humble Adoration and Prideful Expectation

This scene reveals a clear division between two types of individuals: those who approach Christ with humility, acknowledging their need for a Savior, and those who, in their pride, expect Jesus to fit into their personal expectations and standards. The Pharisee's anger in this account is not only tied to the perceived breach of his authority within his own home but also serves as an example of the anger that arises when others do not meet our personal expectations or challenge our sense of control.

Salt is good, but if it loses its saltiness, with what will you

season it? Have salt among yourselves, and be at peace with one another."
(Mark 9:50)

Pride as the Root of Anger

Personal experience affirms this truth: when misunderstandings or offenses occur and anger surfaces, it is often pride that lies at the core. God, in His mercy, gently exposes this pride. For example, when someone criticized my work, I immediately felt offended and angry. Upon reflection, however, I recognized that my reaction was rooted in pride rather than genuine injustice. Such moments reveal how easily pride can fuel anger and hinder spiritual growth.

For all that is in the world—the desires of the flesh and the desires of the eyes and pride of life—is not from the Father but is from the world (1 John 2:16)

Surrendering to God's Healing

Admitting our unrighteousness is a difficult but necessary step. It is beneficial to yield to God, allowing Him to address the deeper issues within. Only He has the power to remove the "cancer" of ill temper from our lives. This process requires a willingness to confess our failures and to let the Holy Spirit reveal and correct the pride that so often drives our reactions. Through humility and honest self-examination, God can transform our hearts and free us from the destructive power of pride-fueled anger. ----

"I will give you a new heart and put a new spirit in you; I will remove from you your heart of stone and give you a heart of flesh."
– (Ezekiel 36:26)

Examples from Scripture: Eliab

Now Eliab his oldest brother heard when he spoke to the men; and Eliab's anger aroused against David, proclaimed:

"Why did you come down here? And with whom have you left those few sheep in the wilderness? I know your pride and the insolence of your heart, for you have come down to see the battle."
And David said, "What have I done now? Is there not a cause?" Then he turned from him toward another and said the same thing; and these people answered him as the first ones did.
(1 Samuel 17:28-30)

Eliab's Pride and the Suppression of Zeal

Eliab's anger toward David for questioning Goliath's taunts serves as a striking example of how pride can manifest when someone else steps out in faith while we ourselves remain unwilling. Confronted by his younger brother's boldness and zeal, Eliab responded not with support or encouragement, but by lashing out and accusing David of insolence and wickedness. This reaction was not simply about David's words or actions, but about the conviction Eliab felt in his own spirit, exposed by David's courageous faith. -----

"Above all, you must understand that in the last days scoffers will come, scoffing and following their own evil desires."
– (2 Peter 3:3)

Such dynamics are still present today. When individuals challenge our spiritual complacency by demonstrating fervor or taking bold steps of faith, it can provoke discomfort or even offense within us. Rather than encouraging the zeal of others, pride often leads us to criticize or attempt to suppress their enthusiasm for God. In Eliab's case, his pride caused him to try to send David away, choosing to cling to defeat rather than humbling himself to support a faithful act. This illustrates how pride, left unchecked, can distort our perspective, making us prefer the status quo over the humility required to embrace and celebrate the spiritual growth of those around us. ---

"A fool finds pleasure in wicked schemes, but a person of understanding delights in wisdom."
– (Proverbs 10:23)

Confronting the Sin of Attacking Zeal

The tendency to react harshly or attack others for their spiritual passion is not unique to Eliab; people respond similarly when their deeply held beliefs or comfort zones are challenged. Such behavior is a sin against God, as it seeks to suppress the zeal and earnestness that should be encouraged among believers. Instead of fostering unity and growth, attacking others for their spiritual fervor creates division and hinders the work of God in the community. ----

"Do not be deceived: God cannot be mocked. A man reaps what he sows."
– (Galatians 6:7)

Acknowledging Our Weakness

The first step toward overcoming this destructive pattern is to admit our own shortcomings. Recognizing the presence of ill temper within ourselves can be a humble experience, but it is necessary if we wish to address the root causes, most notably, pride. Honest self-examination allows us to see how our reactions are often rooted in a desire for self-justification or superiority rather than a genuine concern for truth or unity. Without this honesty, the destructive power of ill temper will continue to undermine our relationships, damage our witness, and inhibit our spiritual growth. True victory over these tendencies begins when we courageously confess our faults, inviting God to work in our hearts. As we allow Him to address the underlying issues and transform us, we become better equipped to respond to others with humility and grace. ---

**"And the grace of our Lord was exceeding abundant with faith and love which is in Christ Jesus."
(1 Timothy 1:14)**

The Lesson of the Pharisee and the Tax Collector

Self-Righteousness and Humility in Prayer

The biblical account of the Pharisee and the tax collector praying in the temple illustrates the danger of self-righteousness and the folly of elevating oneself above others. This attitude, where one considers themselves superior, still manifests in modern places of worship and even on television, where charismatic preachers attract followers with confident, but deceptive, messages. These so-called prophets speak to God as if He were merely a peer, using casual and irreverent language in their sermons. Their aim seems to be to captivate and mislead unsuspecting people, presenting themselves as spiritually elevated above everyone else.

The Deception of False Prophets

These men and women lack any true understanding of God's holiness. Their arrogance is like a dry desert wind, deceptive and empty. If they genuinely sought truth, they would respond as the tax collector did—recognizing their own failings and approaching God with humility. They would echo Isaiah's cry upon glimpsing the presence of God:

Then said I, Woe is me! for I am undone; because I am a man of unclean lips, and I dwell in the midst of a people of unclean lips: for mine eyes have seen the King, the Lord of hosts.
(Isaiah 5:9)

Who can stand in his presence, and boast? Only evil hearts, only those who live in pride, destroying the lives of others. Those who follow these thieves often find out too late, causing such bitterness and rage within their hearts. They walk away from the Lord they never knew. The tax collector exposed to his wrongs, his heart cried out in repentance and sorrow, this alone brings victory, this alone opens the once cold heart to the Love of Christ.

The Folly of Pride and the Power of Humility

In the presence of God, who can truly boast? Only those with hardened hearts, consumed by pride, attempt to do so. These individuals allow arrogance to rule their lives, often hurting others in the process. Tragically, those drawn in by such prideful leaders eventually discover the truth too late, experiencing deep bitterness and anger as a result. This disillusionment can lead them away from a genuine relationship with the Lord—a relationship they never utterly understood. In contrast, the tax collector recognized his faults and, deeply aware of his sin, responded with heartfelt repentance and sorrow. It is this honest humility and turning to God that brings true victory and opens even the coldest heart to the transformative love of Christ. ---

*He also told this parable
to some who trusted in
themselves that they were
righteous and regarded others
with contempt: 'Two men went
up to the temple to pray, one
a Pharisee and the other a
tax-collector. The Pharisee,
standing by himself, was
praying thus, "God, I thank you
that I am not like other people:
thieves, rogues, adulterers,
or even like this tax-collector.
I fast twice a week; I give a
tenth of all my income." But
the tax-collector, standing far
off, would not even look up
to heaven, but was beating
his breast and saying, "God,
be merciful to me, a sinner!"
I tell you, this man went
down to his home justified
rather than the other; for all
who exalt themselves will be
humbled, but all who humble
themselves will be exalted.'
(Luke 18-9-14)*

The Danger of a "Holier Than Thou" Attitude

Adopting a self-righteous or "holier than thou" mindset is deeply offensive to God and marks a heart deceived by pride. Scripture warns against this attitude, describing those who separate themselves and look down on others as "smoke in My nostrils, a fire that burns all day." Such self-exaltation not only invites God's displeasure but also leads to His eventual judgment, as He promises to repay those who persist in this sin.

Who say, 'Keep to yourself, Do not come near me, For I am holier than you! 'These are smoke in My nostrils, A fire that burns all the day. "Behold, it is written

before Me: I will not keep
silence, but will repay—Even
repay into their bosom
— (Isaiah 65:5-6)

Honesty and Transformation: Overcoming Ill Temper

Honesty is essential in the journey to overcome ill temper. Without the willingness to acknowledge our weaknesses, the destructive force of ill temper will persist in our lives. This persistent negativity undermines the quality of our relationships, damages our ability to be a positive influence on others, and hinders our spiritual development. The first step toward real victory over these harmful tendencies is to bravely admit our faults. When we confess our shortcomings and invite God to work in our hearts, we open ourselves to true change and healing. Allowing God to address the root issues and transform our inner selves equips us to interact with others from a place of humility and grace, rather than pride or defensiveness. ----

"But I tell you, love your enemies and pray for those who persecute you."
– (Matthew 5:44)

Ill Temper and the Destructive Power of Gossip the Poisonous Effects of an Uncontrolled Tongue

An ill temper serves as fertile ground for the spread of gossip, transforming relationships and communities into cesspools of bitterness. When anger wielded as a weapon, it destroys not only individual lives but the very fabric of fellowship. The one who cannot control their tongue becomes, in effect, a destructive force—judging others relentlessly while refusing to examine their own soul. Such a person rarely looks inward, failing to recognize their role in the discord that surrounds them.

*To start a quarrel is to release
a flood; so abandon the
dispute before it breaks out.
(<u>Proverbs 17:14</u>)*

Vengeance, Bitterness, and Spiritual Isolation

When vengeance becomes a way of life, it ceases to be life at all. Instead, it leads to a downward spiral—a pit into which the bitter-hearted fall. Grace becomes a distant concept, absent from the heart, leaving the soul wandering in a desert without rest or refreshment. The urge for retaliation and judgment separates a person from the peace and goodness that God intends.

But you, O man of God, flee from these things and pursue righteousness, godliness, faith, love, perseverance, and gentleness.
(1 Timothy 6:11)

The Scriptural Warning Against Bitterness

Scripture warns us to avoid the bitter-hearted, for their presence can defile many souls. The root of bitterness springs up and causes trouble, spreading its poison throughout the community. There is "no fire to warm yourself by" in the company of an embittered soul; such a person drives away goodness and brings only spiritual death.

To start a quarrel is to release a flood; so abandon the dispute before it breaks out.
(Proverbs 17:14)

A Call to Pursue Peace and Grace

We are called to pursue peace with all people to seek sanctification; without this, no one will see the Lord. It is essential to ensure that no one falls short of God's grace, that no root of bitterness allowed to take hold, so that others not defiled by its effects. -

Pursue peace with all men, and the sanctification without which no one will see the Lord. See to it that no one comes short of the grace of God; that no root of bitterness springing up causes trouble, and by it many be defiled. (Hebrews 12:14-15)

Pride, Leadership, and Division in Christian Community

Those who choose to set themselves apart from the rest of the community often act out of pride and a sense of bondage, rather than genuine love. This separation is not rooted in a desire to serve others or foster unity but rather stems from self-centered motives that harm the fellowship. When members of a group question leaders who display authoritarian or dictatorial behavior, they frequently encounter ostracism. Such exclusion is a clear sign of pride and ill temper within those in leadership, rather than an expression of true Christianity. ----

True Christian leadership marked by humility, openness, a willingness to serve rather than dominate. When leaders respond to honest questions or concerns with anger and exclusion, they reveal a spirit that is contrary to the teachings of Christ. The presence of pride and ill temper within leadership not only damages individual relationships but also undermines the unity and spiritual health of the entire community. Rather than fostering an environment of love and mutual encouragement, these attitudes create division and discourage honest dialogue, which are essential for growth and genuine fellowship. This spirit is a stench to God. ---

*you look out not only for his
own interests, but also for
the interests of others.
(Philippians 2:3-4)*

Pride, Group Identity, and the Danger of Seeking Followers.

It is common for individuals to join groups not simply for fellowship, but to elevate themselves above others. This behavior mirrors the prideful ambition of Satan, who, driven by arrogance and a desire for followers, sought to exalt himself. Such motives are rooted in self-centeredness rather than genuine love or unity, and they often lead to division and conflict within the body of Christ. When group identity shifts from a foundation of humility and service to a tool for self-promotion, the spirit of pride begins to flourish. Instead of encouraging one another and fostering genuine fellowship, members may become preoccupied with seeking validation, authority, or recognition. This motivation mirrors the same desire for status that led Satan astray, turning group affiliation into a platform for personal elevation rather than collective growth. Such pursuits inevitably breed exclusion and rivalry within the community. The drive for status can create divisions, as individuals compete for prominence and recognition, rather than working together in humility. This competitive atmosphere fosters a "holier than thou" attitude, in which they set themselves apart as more righteous or superior to others. Not only is this displeasing to God, but it also undermines the true spirit of Christian fellowship, marked by unity, love, and mutual encouragement. ---

**A new command I give you: Love one another. As I have loved you, so you must love one another. By this everyone will know that you are my disciples, if you love one another."
(John 13:34-35)**

The Joy in the Journey of the Redeemed Soul

Grace for the Repentant Heart

When the light of God shines upon a heart that is truly repentant, sorrow for past   into a stream of grace—a crystal river that cleanses the stains of bitterness and the darkness brought by an ill temper. In this moment, the soul no longer imprisoned in the shadows now clothed with righteousness, stepping out of the tomb of darkness into the mercy of the Son of righteousness. The old have passed away, and all things become new.

Therefore, if anyone is in Christ, he is a new creation; old things have passed away; behold, all things have become new. (2 Corinthians 5:17)

A New Beginning in Christ

This is the saving life offered through Jesus Christ. He stands at the door of each heart, inviting all to come to the Cross, where death is left behind and true life begins. Today is the day of salvation. A new beginning is possible for all who answer His call. The only barrier to victory is the unwillingness to let go of self-righteous arrogance. Surrendering to His grace opens the way to transformation and joy for the redeemed soul.

I have been crucified with Christ and I no longer live, but Christ lives in me. The life I now live in the body, I live by faith in the Son of God, who loved me and gave himself for me.
(Galatians 2:20)

www.ingramcontent.com/pod-product-compliance
Lightning Source LLC
Chambersburg PA
CBHW022122150726
47990CB00003B/1469